Tails Are Wagging for Hollyw

"Five paws up for *Hollywood Barks*. Kathryn Segura hits "the mark" on telling the stories of well-known movie dogs and describing how they learn their roles. The training tips from expert trainer Segura can be used with all dogs, whether you want your dog to be a star or a well-mannered pet." -*Mary R. Burch, PhD, Director, Canine Good Citizen & AKC S.T.A.R. Puppy*

"First off, *Hollywood Barks* is an easy read, the pictures are great at chronicling the stories, and this is a world we think we know - but really don't. Kathryn is very humble in this book and people do not realize how much work goes into what she does on set. As movie buff and dog owner - this book gives insight into how movies are made, the detail that goes into some of the most famous pet scenes in cinema, and at the same time gives you lessons you can use at home with your own dog." -*Gregg Champion, President, Champion Media & Entertainment*

"I've known Kathryn since childhood and watched happily from the sidelines as her love of animals became a successful, full time career. With *Hollywood Barks* Kathryn has written her story with the same humorous, loving and passionate touch that she uses with all of her furry friends. I loved this book." -*Richard Holland, Producer and writer*

"*Hollywood Barks* is charming, warm, funny, and poignant. The stories flow effortlessly and they are about people we all know. As an actor, reading *Hollywood Barks* is like reminiscing with an intimate friend while having a cup of hot chocolate. Kathryn Segura is a marvelous storyteller and she has made my gift shopping much easier this year... Thanks Kath!" -*Guich Koock, Actor*

HOLLYW**🐾🐾**D BARKS!

The Tails Behind Famous Dogs, Their Co-Stars,
and Their Companions

Happy™
Tails
Books

A portion of proceeds from this book
is donated to dog rescue organizations

By Kathryn Segura

HOLLYWOOD BARKS!

The Tails Behind Famous Dogs, Their Co-Stars, and Their Human Companions by Kathryn Segura

Published by Happy Tails Books™, LLC www.happytailsbooks.com.

Edited by Kyla Duffy and Lowrey Mumford.

A complete list of photo credits is available on page 109.

Publishers Cataloging In Publication

Hollywood Barks! The Tails Behind Famous Dogs, Their Co-Stars, and Their Human Companions / By Kathryn Segura.

p. ; cm.

ISBN: 978-0-9824895-5-0

1. Hollywood. 2. Dog training 3. Dogs – Behavior. 4. Dog Rescue. 5. Dog Show. I. Segura, Kathryn. II. Title.

SF426.5   2010

636.70887   2009937469

Acknowledgements

Phil Segura as an extra in "Indecent Proposal"

I'm grateful to my parents, Christie Rhodes and Phil Segura, for introducing me to the joy and love animals give their humans. We always had animals in our home, and from my earliest days my parents taught me how to properly handle and care for our pets. Although my mother was stricken with Multiple Sclerosis in her late forties, she still worked diligently to help me grow my business, *PHD Animals*, and was instrumental in its success. My father worked in props and then studio photography, and he was always there to support me when my work became challenging. Both parents were wonderful and are sincerely missed.

I'm lucky to have so much love and support from my brother Mike, my sister-in-law Lisa, and the best nephew and niece ever, Jonathan and Rebecca. They all mean the world to me. I would also like to acknowledge the humans and their K9 stars who helped me make *Hollywood Barks* possible, and thank the wonderful producers, actors, and directors I've been so blessed to work with.

Finally, this book couldn't have happened without my sweet Chloe'; she showed me just how much you get back from giving a rescue dog a forever home.

Paws for Life,

Kathryn

Table of Contents

Foreword 9

Introduction 13

Preface: Fido on Film 101 17

Chapter 1: The Swan that Shaped My Life 21

Behaviors with Bailey: Tips and Terminology 27

Chapter 2: The Swan that Shaped My Life, #2 29

Behaviors with Bailey – "Mark" 34

Chapter 3: Reasonable Doubts about Kennel Care 37

Behaviors with Bailey – "Crawl" 42

Chapter 4: Finding My Heart at the Burbank Shelter 45

Behaviors with Bailey – "Leave It" 51

Chapter 5: Finding Puffy 53

Behaviors with Bailey – "Get It" 58

Chapter 6: Sure, I Do Stunt Work... 61

Behaviors with Bailey – "Head Down" 64

Chapter 7: Even the Smartest Dogs Are Like Children 67

Behaviors with Bailey – "On Your Feet" 70

Chapter 8: Dog Magnet 73

Behaviors with Bailey – "Nudge" 77

Chapter 9: A Pup Takes Flight 79

Behaviors with Bailey – "Go With" 82

Chapter 10: Batteries Not Included 85

Behaviors with Bailey – "Cover" 87

Chapter 11: Setiquette 89

Behaviors with Bailey – "Whistle Recall" 92

Chapter 12: Dogs Sell 95

Behaviors with Bailey – "Give Paw" 100

Chapter 13: Giving 103

Behaviors with Bailey – "Crate Training" 104

Chapter 14: That's a Wrap 107

Photo Credits 109

About Kathryn Segura 111

Mouse, aka "Puffy," and Lin Shaye, aka "Magda", on location for "Behind the Zipper"
(an extra feature on the Director's cut DVD of "There's Something About Mary")

It was an exciting day on the set of *There's Something About Mary*. I was in Florida a day or two before the real shoot began because the special effects guys were still experimenting with my character Magda's beef jerky-looking make-up. As a dog lover with two wonderful Border Collies of my own, I was especially energized about meeting Magda's dog, which was to be a cute, little furball named "Puffy" (or furballs, I should say, as there were to be several dogs playing Puffy).

As I walked onto the set I noticed a woman with a head of beautiful, long, dark hair who had her back to me. It was Kathryn, and I knew my introduction to the pups would be coming soon. With a name like "Puffy," I just assumed Kathryn had some fluffy little poodles for us. But then I saw them peeking over her shoulder – two erect, funny-looking, shaggy ears. "Hmm," I thought, "Maybe *not* poodles."

Kathryn didn't make me wonder for long. She turned around, and with her big, warm smile and sparkling eyes (which I couldn't help notice had a hint of mischief in them) she said, "Hi, *Magda*! Meet your new dog, *Puffy*, aka Slammer. Puffy is a Border Terrier. Say hi, Slammer!"

Well, this certainly wasn't a poodle. As if on cue, Slammer gave me a bark, and I swear, I think she winked. I sat down on the floor as Slammer (aka Puffy) climbed into my lap, sniffed me all over, and then gave me one of her trademark kisses. Kathryn seemed pleased, I was in love, and Slammer was in all her glory. From that moment on, Kathryn, "Puffy," and I were bound to be friends for life.

Kathryn had definitely picked a winner with Slammer which I came to find out is the norm for her. She has an uncanny talent for finding animals with the necessary physical cuteness and unique abilities for each job. Kathryn does not go for the obvious, she goes for the best, and she always nails the right mindset and willingness to perform. The careful thought she puts into each animal selection is what makes her a cut above the rest of her field.

Lin Shaye

Sure, Puffy could have been a poodle, but the performance would never have turned out as good as it did, and our kissing/make-out scene would probably have not gained a permanent spot in film history (Border Terriers are extraordinary kissers). Like the animal actors she has a special "eye and nose for," Kathryn is the "unusual best," which makes her a joy to work with. -*Lin Shaye, Actress*

Bailey and Holly with their "mom," Kathryn Segura

Introduction

Don't feel bad if you've never heard of a studio wrangler. Not many people have, which means we are doing our job well. We are the unseen, the phantasms, essential beings that lurk in the shadows off-camera, ensuring animal welfare and a flawless performance. If there is an animal on set, so are we.

My personal experience with animal training began long ago. As a child I was always involved with showing dogs in breed conformation and obedience, but it wasn't until I was well into my adulthood that training animals became my occupation. I was heading towards a career in high fashion make-up when my life took some interesting twists and turns. The path led to a career in animal training over 20 years ago, and I've never looked back.

My parents had a hunch that my life would go to the dogs from the very start, as I was born with a paw print on my thigh. It's true! They had a Golden Retriever who loved to dance, but of course, my mom stopped dancing with him towards the end of her pregnancy. Just before my big debut, Mom mistakenly made a gesture the dog interpreted as a sign to start dancing. He jumped towards her, and his front paws came down on her stomach. Two weeks later I was born with a paw print on my thigh. The doctor said it would be gone by the time I was one, and although the mark has disappeared from my leg, it has clearly stayed with me in my heart.

The animals in my life have since taken me on a grand adventure through the challenging universe of dog shows and the magical world of Hollywood. The glamour and glitz of it all, coupled with the lasting friendships (K9 and human) I've established, have afforded me a lifestyle that most people only dream of – and I am grateful. My work has also put me in a position to give back to the animals that have shaped my life. I seem to be a magnet for dogs in need, and finding them homes and a better life has been one of the most rewarding aspects of my career.

They say every dog has his day, but usually it's the human actors that get all the recognition. I wrote this book to honor the K9 actors I've worked with and to share their amazing tales. I've also included a Hollywood training tip at the end of each chapter for you and your dog to enjoy. Remember, our dogs live to please us, and when you teach your dog and praise him for learning, you've made him very happy. Most dogs need a job, which can be anything, from basic obedience behaviors (sit, stay, come…) to agility or herding. Your dog is probably no exception. Why not give him his 15 seconds of fame by teaching him some tricks you can show off together? He'll love it, and I bet you'll be smiling, too!

Now without further adieu, here are the stories of some amazing working dogs, their famous co-stars, and their human companions who have all touched my life. Enjoy!

Kathryn Segura

Commercial shoot in downtown L.A.

Preface: Fido on Film 101

Few people can answer trivia questions about the actual work dogs do in Hollywood, so here's a bit of an introduction. Any dog you've ever seen in a television show, commercial, or film has a human studio wrangler (trainer) hiding in the shadows. We serve as dog-directors – the director directs us and then we direct the dogs. Confused? It's not really as complicated as it sounds.

As studio wranglers we develop strong bonds with our animals, and our love for them drives us to do all we can to ensure their happiness and welfare. In return, we expect our dogs to understand our signs and signals and to perform to the best of their abilities. This may sound silly, but dogs are very intelligent, talented creatures who can do much more than most people give them credit for. So that's our job – to help animals exercise their full potential in a safe, productive environment.

Not only are there at least one or two trainers on set, the AHA (American Humane Association), a non-profit oversight committee that serves as advocate and protector of animal actors, is also present. Starting in 1925, the AHA unofficially monitored animal safety on movie sets. It wasn't until a horse fell to its death in the 1929 filming of *Jessie James* that public outrage catalyzed a re-thinking of animal safety in film. In 1930 the AHA's role in animal advocacy was legitimized, and now an AHA presence is an official requirement for every set that involves an animal. When you see "NO ANIMAL WAS HARMED IN THE MAKING OF THIS FILM" at the end of film credits, you are seeing the AHA stamp of approval.

The Chinese Zodiac may call 1930 the year of the horse (which I guess it was, since the horse that died was avenged). I think it was the year of the dog in Hollywood. Warner Brothers Studios was in a dilemma - they needed a hit movie, but because they were just getting started, they didn't have the funds to hire a top "star." They were on a wing and a prayer...until their salvation came in the form of four paws and a loud bark.

Rin Tin Tin

In September of 1930, Warner Brothers received a script entitled *The Wonder Dog*, a true story about a man and his dog during World War I. The man was an American serviceman named Lee Duncan, and the dog was a German Shepherd he rescued from a bombed-out kennel in France. Sound familiar? The film was released as *Rin Tin Tin*. It became such an American classic that even today, 80 years later, the film still has an active fan club.

My friends, that is when dogs first "got their day" on the silver screen, and on many occasions they've continued to be Hollywood's rainmakers.

Ace: "When is someone going to bring me that cheese plate?"

The Swan that Shaped My Life

As a family, we already had a female sable and white Shetland Sheepdog (Sheltie) named Pitsie. And although I showed her in obedience trials and won many Junior Handling awards with her, I felt I was ready for my *own* dog. Many 12-year-olds *say* they want a puppy to train. They then forget about it within months and the burden of care falls to mom. Not me – I was serious. It was time I stepped up my game.

One day my mom took me to a dog show, where I saw a beautiful Sheltie named Astronaut win "Best of Breed." We congratulated the owners, who informed us that Astronaut had recently sired a litter. They invited us to meet the puppies, and of course, we jumped at the chance.

At four weeks old the puppies were all precious, but after one look at a little, tri-colored male, I knew he was the one. I promised my mother I'd pay with my own money, and we struck an unimaginable deal with the owners. It turns out they thought he was *ugly*, and so they gave him to me for next to nothing – the son of a purebred champion! I don't know why or how, but I saw something different in the "ugly" dog who I immediately named Ace. Even if he wasn't the most attractive puppy, I knew he'd grow into a swan. So after waiting four incredibly long weeks (it's never good to wean puppies too soon), Ace came home.

You know where this story is going – Ace did turn into the swan I had dreamed he would become. He was so handsome that I showed him in conformation classes, and he became an AKC breed champion. I also trained him in obedience, but unlike Pitsie, he hated the trials.

Shortly thereafter, I met a trainer at a pet expo who gave me some studio training tips. I found that Ace loved learning the studio behaviors, and he seemed to have the necessary attributes to become a dog "star," but school prevented me from pursuing film work for him. We were kind of stuck – like being all dressed up with nowhere to go.

Then a call came in from Betsy, my mother's best childhood friend, and along with it came an unexpected opportunity. Betsy's husband Bob was the head writer on a soap opera in New York, and Bob's friend in California was the producer on the soap *Return to Peyton Place*. The California producer had recently told Bob he needed a Sheltie for a scene (they were his favorite breed), and Betsy and Bob had immediately thought of us. They must have really laid it on thick when they told the producer about Ace because, sight unseen, he was hired.

At the time, my father was a studio photographer who was conveniently shooting at NBC Studios in Burbank where *Return to Peyton Place* was being filmed. Every day for a week he took Ace and me to work. Meeting the cast and crew and getting paid to "play with my dog" was exhilarating. I'll never forget our first day: there I was, peering over the director's shoulder as he and the actors sat around a table discussing the script, including the parts that called for Ace. (I later came to learn this is called a "table read" – an essential daily huddle where everyone gets together and strategizes about the shoot.) Upon hearing Ace's name mentioned, I could feel the magic of Hollywood like a tingling sensation in my soul – Ace and I were about to make our big break.

When the cameras started rolling, I wasn't really sure what I was supposed to do. I figured I should just make sure that Ace was on his mark, and I was out of frame. A few minutes into it, the director told Ace to do something and Ace did it – which seemed reasonable. The director directs *all* of the action, no? It wasn't until he said, "I can't believe I just gave a dog direction and he did it...correctly," that I found out I was the one who was supposed to communicate with Ace. It's like playing "telephone." On the set, the director talks with the trainer, and the trainer talks to the animal actor. Hey, no sweat. My dog's so smart that the director can talk directly to him... (Oh, wait, scratch that. Where would that leave me?)

Ace turned out to be a great actor, easily taking direction and always looking natural, but not everything about our first shoot went smoothly. For example, one day during lunch Dad and I put Ace in his dressing room (real stars, like Ace, get dressing rooms), and we went to eat in the cafeteria. When we returned, the door had automatically locked from the inside, and poor Ace had become trapped. Panicking, I waited in front of the room while Dad went to find help or a key. My anxiety doubled when Ace was requested on the set over the loudspeaker. Now not only was my dog stuck, but he also had somewhere to be. After what seemed like forever, Dad finally returned with someone who could unlock the door. While I may have been a bit frazzled, Ace was fine and we were back in action.

Ace - the perfect family dog, on the set of "Return to Peyton Place"

Ace and I loved our 15 seconds of fame, but we didn't do much after the *Return to Peyton Place* shoot. Instead we kept up with dog shows – even after my mother took Pitsie, Ace, and me to Madrid, Spain, for her new job. What a learning experience! The difference between showing dogs in Spain and showing dogs in the States is as vast as the ocean is deep. If you ever saw the movie *Best in Show*, well, let's just say it's an *understatement* of what really goes on here. American dogs are groomed to the nines, and when they go into the ring with their handlers, everyone sits politely, silently watching the judging. In contrast, Spanish dogs come out looking as if they had just herded some bulls through the streets, and the crowd goes wild. Spectators run around the outside of the ring, yelling and clapping - anything to get their favorite dog's attention. Spanish exuberance does not end with fútbol (soccer); evidently it extends to dog shows, too.

Needless to say, Spanish show rules are very different American ones, but Ace adapted just fine. Well, better than fine, I guess – *he* did become a Spanish Champion. His success led to a TV appearance for both Ace and Pitsie on a very popular show called *Zoo Loco* (Zoo Crazy). Our job was to introduce the Shetland Sheepdog breed to Spain. The popularity of the show blew me away. After the segment aired, I couldn't walk the dogs without a mob follow us yelling, "Zoo Loco!" I felt like I walking Penélope Cruz and Antonio Banderas on leash.

When we moved back to California, Ace retired and I went to college. In school I became very interested in make-up, taking a theatrical make-up course from a professor who was also a studio make-up artist. Upon deciding that studio make-up was also my calling, I apprenticed and then took a make-up union test, which I passed. I worked as a make-up artist for two years until a strike left us all without jobs.

Fortunately an opportunity arose with Lancôme, and I was again swept away to Europe. Because Ace was older now and had a heart murmur, as a family we decided he should remain in my mother's care this time. I missed him desperately but the Lancôme high fashion make-up opportunity was irresistible. I put a photo of Ace on my make-up case, and he stayed with me there, and in my heart, wherever I went.

The day before I came home from my year abroad, Ace tragically passed away. I couldn't imagine a more cheerless homecoming.

As we all know, our furry family members never live long enough. A dear friend said that unless we have parrots or tortoises for pets, our hearts will be repeatedly broken. So true – dogs and cats are like toddlers who never grow up and then die. Every moment together is so worth the anguish, but their inevitable passing dreadfully looms at the same time.

I picked up the pieces after my brokenhearted homecoming, realizing I needed a career change. In the year I was gone I had lost my passion for studio make-up, and since Los Angeles is no Paris, my high fashion work was relegated to a sparse few print jobs. Noticing my frustration (and dwindling bank account), my mother suggested I resume dog training. She was right – it was time for a new puppy...

Behaviors with Bailey: Tips and Terminology

My dog Bailey and I love working together on new behaviors, which is something you can enjoy with your dog, too! There's nothing more fun than sharing in the learning process (except, maybe, watching your dog perform what you've taught him). After each chapter in this book I've included a training tip you can try with your own dog. Read through the whole tip first to be sure you understand the process. But before we begin, here are some general tips on terminology commonly used in dog training:

- ❧ **Bait:** Treats, food, or toys – whatever you can use as a reward that motivates your dog

- ❧ **Bait Bag:** A fanny pack or small bag, worn at the waist, containing dog treats

- ❧ **Pay:** To give your dog a treat for performing the behavior you want from him

- ❧ **To "have a behavior:"** This phrase means that the dog can consistently perform a particular behavior

- ❧ **Treats:** Don't over-treat your dog. When possible, reward him with just praise – lots of it! When you are treating him, consider healthy rewards like small chicken pieces cooked with garlic, bits of a Dick Van Patten's Natural Balance roll (my favorite – if you don't know them, they're meal tubes that can be cut into small pieces), or cleaned, raw carrots.

The training tips contained herein assume your dog already knows basic obedience behaviors such as "sit," "stay," "come," "release," and "down." For tips on training these behaviors, please visit http://happytailsbooks.com/hollywood.htm.

Tasha, Beverly Hills Dog Show, scent hurdling competition

The Swan that Shaped My Life, #2

Have you ever had a pet die and missed him so badly that you wanted the exact same dog? Perhaps you even named your new dog "(dog's name here) #2?" Well, I didn't go that far, but when my mom suggested I get back into training, I definitely had a strong urge to get a male, tri-colored Shetland Sheepdog - I wasn't being picky or anything. After a month or so of searching, I found a litter of tri-colored Shelties, including two males. I went over to see the puppies and picked up a cute little guy who settled right into my lap. So sweet, giving kisses with that wonderful puppy breath. I'll take hi…. What's this? Suddenly out of nowhere, another feisty furball unceremoniously evicts my sweet boy from my lap and stakes her claim. What choice did I have? The one I took home turned out to be a "she" who I named Totally Tasha. (Give me a break. It was "totally" the 1980's.)

Tasha loved to learn, and learn she did. Obedience was a breeze, and our growing bond rejuvenated me. It took only three shows for her receive her Companion Dog AKC certification (an obedience award), and she always placed in the top four (usually first) in competition. I then started training her on studio behaviors as I had Ace. We'd train at home, and once she had it down I'd take her to the park for added distractions.

One day at the park we saw a group of people working with their dogs on some sort of course. I watched as the dogs ran, one at a time, over four hurdles. After the last hurdle there was a flat board with four numbered dumbbells on it. The dog would sniff the dumbbells, pick one out, and then run back over the hurdles, proudly carrying the dumbbell. Was our park the new Venice Beach for dogs? I had no idea what this was, but Tasha wanted in on the act.

I came to find out the dogs were not weightlifting. They were scent hurdling, an activity that requires agility, speed, and smarts. The goal is for the dog to choose the dumbbell with his handler's scent on it. He then must return it to his handler in the fastest possible time. In competition, the dogs and handlers wear racing vests with a number on it, and the correct dumbbell is also numbered accordingly. This way, the judges can easily tell if the dog chooses the right dumbbell. Teams of four send two dogs over the hurdles at a time. The first team that gets all four dogs back with the correct dumbbells wins.

Tasha with all her trophies

I was curious about Tasha's enthusiasm so my new friends encouraged me to let her give it a try. Leashed, I walked her over the jumps and showed her where the dumbbell was. Then I took off her leash and sent her on her own. Bless her heart, she did it all on the first try and ran back to me with the correct dumbbell. The astonished handlers immediately recruited us, noting that training a dog for scent hurdling usually takes six months to a year.

In less than a week we had our first race, and our team won. Not only did Tasha pick up the sport quickly, she was one of the fastest dogs competing. People noticed Tasha's talent and began asking me to train their dogs, which is when my life really took an interesting new turn.

I asked for, and received, approval to teach obedience classes in the park. I called my business PHD (Perfect House Dog), and with that my career as a trainer and studio wrangler began. You see, I lucked out. The studio behavior classes I hosted exposed me to a new group of people in the TV and film industry who were in need of my skills and connections. Training their dogs wasn't enough; they wanted help finding the right animals for their projects. It took some time for me to realize it, but my whole life had been leading me towards providing people with that sort of assistance. Training and showing dogs had given me a lake-sized pool of talent to draw from, and the ripple effect included introductions to people who could provide other animals, too. PHD grew into more than just behavior classes – it was suddenly an animal agency.

Working with my own dog Tasha, who subsequently appeared in many commercial and print ads, is what solidified my passion for studio training. Our most memorable shoot was a Coors "dog show" commercial. Tasha was recruited along with our dog show friends and their dogs. For me it was like a dream come true - beautiful dogs of different breeds, expertly performing alongside their handlers. The job felt so natural and satisfying, which made me realize that studio wrangling was what I wanted to do with my life.

Tasha with her dog show friends at the Coors commercial shoot

Age didn't stop Tasha but insensible photographers did. When she was nine years old she was hired for a dog food ad, and we went to the photographer's studio for the shoot. He photographed Tasha eating food out of a bowl on the floor for a while, until Tasha got to the point where she was done. She just stopped. I was a little surprised because she could usually work longer, but clearly Tasha was tired and needed a rest. The photographer didn't care and insisted we try once more.

Well, Tasha tried her best but simply couldn't eat more, which made the photographer very impatient. He got up and pushed Tasha's head into the dish. If it were me, I would have bitten him. But Tasha, true professional she was, didn't.

"Take your hands off my dog," I said.

He said, "I need this shot."

I picked up Tasha, got my things, and started to leave – and he had the audacity to ask where I was going. I said, "No one treats an animal like that in front of me."

"You'll never work for me again!" he ranted.

"You've got that right. Lose my number." I was out the door.

After walking off the set, I reported the photographer to the AHA. I'm not sure what they did, but I do know that was his last, or next to last, job working with animals, and it was definitely his last job working with me.

When I got home, I checked Tasha out because she seemed to be acting strangely. I found a lump on her neck and immediately made an appointment with her vet, who kept her overnight and removed the lump to test it. When I picked her up the next day, he said it was a completely encapsulated tumor and that they would have the test results in a few days. I felt encouraged; Tasha was acting more like herself already.

I was working on a set when my mother called to deliver the bad news. Crying, she told me the test results showed thyroid carcinoma. The vet told my mother that Tasha only had three to six months to live, with or without treatment. Devastating though this news seemed, for some reason I knew she was going to be fine. The recommended course of action for Tasha's cancer was radiation treatments but they made her so sick I decided to seek an alternative. An herbalist put together a daily dose of cancer-fighting herbs, and within six or seven months, Tasha was deemed cancer-free and in full remission.

Tasha never worked in print or film after her illness, but she was a wonderful training assistant for PHD. A born natural in showing other dogs the correct execution of behaviors, Tasha was my true partner as our business thrived. In our free time we visited hospitals, and Tasha's survival story served as an inspiration for ailing children and adults.

Tasha did finally pass eight-and-a-half years later at seventeen-and-half-years old to the day, a good age even for a Sheltie. Our activities together filled her life with meaning and purpose, and her presence in my life did the same for me. Tasha fooled most people with her gloomy cancer prognosis but I knew she would be my miracle dog.

Behaviors with Bailey – "Mark"

No, we are not going to teach your dog to pee (mark) all over your house. In studio language a "mark" is the place on stage where an actor is supposed to go when the director says, "Action!" "Mark" is a must-have behavior for studio work, and it's a great way to impress your friends, too.

Goal: To teach your dog to go to a spot on the floor without having to take him there.

Lesson:

- 🐾 Put a large, low box on the floor.

- 🐾 With your dog's leash loosely in hand (and your dog attached to it, of course), walk over to the box.

- 🐾 As soon as your dog touches it, even if it's just a toe, say, "**Mark**," and praise him.

- 🐾 Make him stay there for a second, and then release him.

- 🐾 When you think your dog has it, give the "mark" command when you are only halfway to the box. Reward him with lots of praise when he touches the box.

Intermediate Challenge:

- 🐾 Practice with your dog off leash, allowing him to go ahead of you and saying "mark" when he's almost there. The goal is to get distance between you and your dog.

- 🐾 Continue the training for 10 minutes each day, making the mark smaller and smaller. Eventually, it can be as small as a penny or pebble.

Experts Only:

- 🐾 Put more and more distance between you and your dog, and say, "Mark" as early as you can in the game.

- 🐾 Your goal is to be able to show your dog the mark, say, "Mark," and then have him go to it.

Tips:

- 🐾 Some dogs may want to circle the box. That's ok; your dog will touch it eventually.

- 🐾 Before sending your dog to a mark, always show him where it is at least once by walking him there and giving the "mark" command.

Human Hollywood stars get to live in big, wonderful homes.
Shouldn't K9 actors be afforded the same luxury?

Reasonable Doubts about Kennel Care

I believe a dog is a family member first and foremost. Over the centuries dogs have been domesticated, and most have been bred as companion animals. It's nice when we can find them other jobs to do, like acting or herding, but in the end they should also be allowed to do their job as companions. Many studio animal companies have big properties with kennels for their movie dogs. This may be fine for them, but it's not for me. After a long day on the set my K9 actors go home to their families where they can spend the night happily pushing their humans out of bed.

Though our philosophies may differ, that is not to say all large studio animal companies don't care deeply for their dogs. Early in my career, a well-known trainer with a large kennel retired, and he made the decision to retire his dogs, too. Many other companies would have paid top dollar for them, but he wouldn't even consider passing his dogs along. Instead they all went to loving, private homes where they could live out their days doing all of the wonderful things that pets do. He didn't rest until all of his dogs found loving homes, and I really respect him for that.

The experience of living with a family in a private home prepares a K9 actor for playing the frequently-requested "family dog" role. In my opinion, this is extremely valuable, and I find that dogs who have this opportunity also come to work with an extra sparkle in their eyes. My trainer-friend Gayle Phelps lived with her Golden Retriever, Jon, whose story is a perfect example…

An exciting call came in for a new NBC television series called *Reasonable Doubts.* Mark Harmon and Marlee Matlin were starring, and Mark's character, Detective Dicky Cobb, was to have a dog. I was invited to give a showing so I brought in a variety of dogs, including a three-year-old Golden Retriever named Jon, who put on a wonderful performance. Robert "Bob" Singer, the creator and director of the show, absolutely loved it, and upon hearing Bob's enthusiastic "Good job!" remark, Jon proceeded to bestow slobbery kisses all over the laughing man.

Jon's exuberance landed him the role of the hero dog (dog "star"), and during the two years the show aired, Jon could often be found behind the set playing ball with Mark or Bob. They grew very close and got along like family, which made for a very natural performance for both man and dog. It also set the stage for a cheerful work environment.

Just like humans, animal actors sometimes have sick days or other obligations. Establishing a routine and having a good back-up dog is instrumental in keeping things flowing smoothly. In Jon's case, he was on the small side so his back-up was a female (Golden Retriever fur makes it difficult to tell gender, anyway). She was very good but we didn't need to use her much. Aside from the occasional double-booking, Jon never shut down like some dogs do when they are overwhelmed. He expertly performed his duties as Mark's "family dog," which was no surprise to me since companionship was a "job" he already knew so well.

Jon going to work. Now that's a dog who loves his job!

Ever wonder what goes on behind the scenes of a TV show? Shoots are either on a set (in a studio) or on location (in the "real" world, outside of a studio). You can't always believe what you see - often when you think you're watching something like a scene filmed in a home or on a beach, you're really seeing a studio set. Hollywood employs masters of illusion who can build just about anything, be it a replica of a famous landmark or an invented fantasy landscape.

Unlike movies, TV shows are generally filmed with multiple cameras, shooting the same scene from different angles all at once. They are either filmed in private with only a select few onlookers and crew, or they are shot in front of a live studio audience. From the actor's perspective, there is a big difference between the two. *Reasonable Doubts* was unique because it was a TV series shot at Warner Brothers Studios on a sound stage, but they did it with only one camera and multiple takes, like a film. (Each time the same scene is shot, it is referred to as a "take.")

On the *Reasonable Doubts* set we had no audience, but occasional studio tour trams would pass by. Every once in a while, a few lucky tourists even got to meet the cast and observe us rehearsing (visits were never allowed during the filming of the actual show). The stars were very gracious to the tourists, and the dogs didn't mind much, either. Even so, I always kept the dogs out of petting range to help maintain their focus.

A "live" TV show with an audience is a whole different animal (no pun intended). It's like doing a stage play with cameras and sound booms (microphones) everywhere, stacked on top of the pressure of performing in front of a live audience. For studio wranglers, live shoots are particularly challenging because multiple cameras are filming from many angles, and we, somehow, need to stay out of the shots. As for the actors, let's face it, audiences are distracting. Whispered voices, shuffling feet - these disturbances can throw off actors (K9 and human).

Have you heard the saying "a bombproof horse?" It refers to the kind of animal you need for a live audience shoot, and it must date back to the early Westerns. While the human actors are practicing their lines, the K9 actors are memorizing their behaviors so they are confident and capable when the cameras start to roll. They often can't see the trainer during the filming of the show, so in rehearsal the trainer walks the dog from mark to mark, showing him exactly what he needs to do and when he needs to do it. It's like a memory game for dogs. Because of distractions and complications, dogs hired to perform in front of live studio audiences must truly be the best of the best.

Now that you're "in the know," the next time you see that "filmed before a live studio audience" statement in the opening credits of a show, give the actors (and wranglers) a little extra respect. We were all working especially hard to entertain you.

As you can see, there are many challenges a dog must be ready for on set. Because Jon got to go *home* for a good night's sleep, he arrived on the set in the morning ready for anything. That's the kind of dog I like working with. I've been encouraged to see a significant shift in common industry practices regarding K9 actors over the past twenty years, and now more than ever studio trainers are keeping their dogs in private homes. Some have changed their thinking, but the more obvious reason is economic. Trainers who have large kennels have to pay for the dogs and caretakers whether they are working on not. Trainers that keep a minimal number of dogs in their own home, and then use privately owned dogs when necessary, have significantly less expense. Because this equation adds up favorably for everyone, I hope we'll continue to see a rise in the number of working dogs who live at home.

Behaviors with Bailey – "Crawl"

Teaching your dog to crawl is fun, but note that it's much easier to teach females than males. Why? Let's just say that our little boys' extra parts sometimes get in the way. If your male dog wants to crawl with his butt up in the air – hey, that's great! He's got his own style.

Goal: To teach your dog to crawl.

Lesson:

- 🐾 While on leash, put your dog in a down-stay in front of a chair.
- 🐾 Sit on the opposite side of the chair and gently pull the leash through to you (without pulling on your dog – ever).
- 🐾 Softly say, "Come, crawl," and back up a bit as he comes underneath the chair.
- 🐾 Give lots of praise when your dog accomplishes his task.

Intermediate Challenge:

- 🐾 Once your dog has the hang of it, put another chair in front of the first one so he has further to crawl.
- 🐾 Try it without the leash.

Experts Only:

- 🐾 Practice off leash without out a chair.
- 🐾 Say, "Crawl." If he tries to stand as he comes towards you, hold the treat in front of him and gently place your other hand on his back as you move backwards.
- 🐾 Don't get discouraged – training this behavior can take some practice but it's a great party trick and a fun behavior for your dog to have.

Tips:

- 🐾 Be close to the chair on the other side, so your dog doesn't try to run around it.
- 🐾 If you bait your dog with food, be sure to keep the treat down low in front of him while you back up.
- 🐾 Never pay your dog until he accomplishes his task – if you do, it only reinforces that he doesn't need to do what he is told.

Now go move some furniture and play crawling musical chairs with your dog!

The "Indecent Proposal" zoo scene

Finding My Heart at the Burbank Shelter

At the same time my work with *Reasonable Doubts* was coming to a close, I received a call for the film *Indecent Proposal*, a movie starring Robert Redford, Demi Moore, and Woody Harrelson. I was asked to meet with director Adrian Lyne at Paramount Pictures to discuss exotic animals for a party scene at a zoo. At the end of our discussion Adrian mentioned that he would like to have a dog in the film, even though there wasn't one scripted, and asked if I could I put a showing together for him. How could I say no to that?

I called my animal company and trainer contacts to organize the showing. Adrian and I looked at dogs all day long, but when the last dog left he still seemed unsatisfied. He turned to me and said, "They are all great dogs but not one of them is right. The movie needs a happy, friendly, lovable dog. Could you please go to the shelter and see what you can find there?" Of course!

Off to the Burbank Shelter I went in search of the dog Adrian had described. I found a sweet Pointer mix that fit the bill perfectly. He was very happy and lovable, and after spending some time with him, I thought he might work. I took a couple of pictures and brought them back to Adrian, who responded simply, "Let's get him."

When I called the shelter to see when the Pointer mix would become available for adoption, they told me two days and cautioned me about their first-come, first-serve policy (even for dogs that are to become movie stars). What really surprised me was that, according to the woman on the phone, being at the shelter for their opening at 7:00am would not be enough. If I wanted the dog I should arrive around 2:00 because people park in the lot and wait. "And," she again mentioned, "The first one here gets the dog." Two in the morning, SERIOUSLY?

I took the woman on the phone at her word, and on the eve of my "camping trip" readied myself with everything I would need to survive during the desolate, wee hours in the Burbank Shelter parking lot: coffee (check), pillow (check), nuts (check), cell phone (double-check). My survival kit and I were on the road at 1:30, which put me at the shelter just before two. As I was hunkering down for a long, boring night, I noticed another car already in the lot. I couldn't believe my eyes - was it really possible that someone else also arrived this early for the Pointer pup? That dog must lay golden eggs!

 I called my mother to let her know I arrived safely and to confer with her about the other car. She wasn't worried; her theory was that he just parked there to sleep. Yeah, sure, Mom. That's *exactly* why he was there (not). With no way to know until the shelter opened at seven, I extinguished my campfire (also known as dashboard lights) and spent some time examining the inside of my eyelids.

Around 6:45, a field officer came out to see who was first. There were still only two of us in the parking lot, but it only takes one big wind gust to blow over a camping tent – and my was about to be upended. The man was indeed there for the Pointer mix and had arrived in the parking lot at midnight. He was so happy to get the dog that my disappointment was offset by knowing the Pointer mix was going to a good home. I guess I would just have to pitch another tent.

Little did I know, however, my luck was about to change. Just as I was leaving the shelter, the officer who spent time with the Pointer mix and me on my previous visit pulled me aside, saying, "Please don't leave just yet. Come with me."

So I went. On our walk towards the kennels, she told me a Lab mix was turned in the night before. The dog was an "owner surrender," which meant that because the owner dropped her off and relinquished his ownership rights, she could be adopted immediately.

The first thing this dog did as we approached her kennel was pee all over herself. She wasn't really submissive so much as afraid and confused as to why she was there once again. Apparently this was her third trip to the shelter. The first time she was brought in with her littermates as a six-week-old puppy. The family that adopted her brought her back because "she was getting too big." (Duh – she's a Lab mix.) Then another couple adopted her, but they returned her a week later because the husband got an out-of-state job. Not only did this guy dump the dog, he dumped his wife, too, and said he was going to start a new life without them. (Jerk.) The wife no longer needed the dog. What she needed was a divorce lawyer!

This beautiful, sweet girl, peering sheepishly at me through the chain-link gate, had truly been the victim of a series of unfortunate circumstances. I knew, at that moment, she was going home to live with me forever, whether Adrian chose her for the film or not. While the shelter staff cleaned her up, I filled out the adoption paperwork and walked around looking at other dogs. Without a doubt, this Lab mix was the one.

Chloe' – "Does this collar bring out the color of my eyes?"

When she was ready I told the dog to say goodbye-for-good because she was never going to find herself back at the shelter again. She wagged her tail, jumped into my van, and headed right into the dog crate to lie down. On the way home I decided to name her Chloe' after one of my favorite fragrances because getting her was better than receiving the most perfumed bouquet of flowers. Chloe' and I stopped by the vet for a check-up, and with a clean bill of health we went straight home so she could get started on her new life.

Once home, I called Adrian to tell him what happened with the Pointer mix. Relieved that he couldn't wait to meet Chloe', when we got off the phone I moved on to my second order of business – letting some friends know about the other great shelter dogs I had seen. I immediately talked to my neighbor, and he and his wife went and got one. I also told one of the guys on the film crew, who adopted another. I went there for one Pointer mix which I didn't get, but I ended up finding homes for three other dogs. I would say my "camping" trip was a success!

Adrian liked Chloe' as much as I did and immediately gave her the part. She had never acted before and I had to train her right on the set, so it was a good thing she scored her own trailer, too. Lucky for both of us, it turned out she was a natural.

During the time I was prepping for *Indecent Proposal*, my dad called to say he was bored with retirement and needed something to do. I told him I had just the job for him – he could help me on the movie set. His timing couldn't have been more perfect. With my dad there, Chloe' had a personal photographer, and I had an amazing assistant. My dad didn't only help me, though. He appeared in the *Indecent Proposal* zoo scene as an extra, and while at the zoo he shot a great photograph of some hippos, which ended up being used as decoration in the film.

Each morning Chloe', my dad, and I would arrive on set and go over the script with Adrian, to verify what Chloe' would be doing. Day after day she nailed her behaviors, and everyone loved her (including the camera). Most of her scenes were with Woody Harrelson, who also developed a strong bond with her. After a time, Woody even began calling Chloe' into his trailer while he rehearsed

Chloe' and Woody, million dollar pals

his lines. Her companionship on set was not only reserved for me. In fact, Woody and Chloe' spent so much time together, and had such a good rapport, that many people were convinced she was *his* dog!

If you've seen *Indecent Proposal*, you know that the plot is about a man who offers another man a million dollars to sleep with his wife. The running joke between Woody and me was that Woody would pay me a million dollars to take home my wonderful dog. Trust me, though, even for a million dollars Chloe' wasn't going home with anyone but me (sorry, Woody).

After filming *Indecent Proposal*, Chloe's story was featured in the *Los Angeles Times*. She was the dog who made it from pound puppy to movie star – an inspiration, and a testament to the fact that shelter dogs can thrive when given the chance. Her acting career blossomed, and Chloe' went on to do many commercials and print jobs.

I remember one job in which the trip there was actually more memorable than the shoot. We were headed for a commercial shoot in New Mexico, and on the flight Chloe' got to sit with me in the cabin (in the 90's big dogs could still do that). At 110 pounds she was the size of a human, so it only seemed right that she be treated like one. She loved looking out the window during takeoff and landing and otherwise just slept at my feet. I don't know if she realized she performed as a "therapy dog" on the flight, but she sure helped one terrified woman, who moved to sit next to me (instead of her husband) to pet Chloe' with shaking hands. She thanked us both when we landed, saying it was the best flight she ever had. After that experience, what could I do but get Chloe' certified as a therapy dog?

Chloe' lived a full life, but it was, unfortunately, not a long one. Cancer took her from us at the young age of seven. She died in my arms on Valentine's Day, which was poetic justice since she had a great, big heart and was most definitely the love of my life. If anyone deserves fame, Chloe' does, having gone through such a traumatic puppyhood. When I look back on the night before I met her, camping out in the parking lot of the Burbank shelter and thinking that I was waiting on a Pointer mix, I'm glad that instead Chloe' was waiting on me.

Behaviors with Bailey – "Leave It"

"Leave it" will come in handy in day-to-day living. For example, if you have a dog who goes crazy about every dog you pass when you're out walking, "leave it" works great. It is also used when your dog wants to pick up something or stick his head somewhere he shouldn't. "Leave it" is a mandatory prerequisite for the "get it" behavior you will learn in Chapter Five.

Goal: To teach your dog to let go of, and/or move away from a person or object.

Lesson:

- 🐾 Get in front of your dog with two similar treats or toys.

- 🐾 With one hand, hold the toy or treat in front of your dog, but when he goes to check it out, say, "Leave it."

- 🐾 Once your dog backs away from that hand, praise him and give him the toy/treat from your other hand.

You'll be surprised how quickly your dog catches on to this and how useful you find it in everyday life!

"Puffy" and Cameron Diaz, from "There's Something About Mary"

Finding Puffy

A production company called looking for a toy breed dog for a new Twentieth Century Fox film. When I heard that the Farrelly Brothers (Peter and Bobby) created and were also directing it, I knew it had to be good. The name of the film was *There's Something About Mary*.

The producers requested a small, foofy dog, so I showed them a Toy Poodle and a Papillion. These dogs seemed to impress them, and they gave me a script to review. It was hilarious – I laughed out loud, but as I continued reading, I just couldn't imagine a Toy Poodle being the right fit for the role. The script described a comical "battle" between Ben Stiller's unlucky, love-smitten character, Ted, and Puffy, the dog they were casting. Puffy had to be tough - what they needed was a Terrier who could handle the physical behaviors the script required, including dragging Ted across the room by his leg as he struggled to get away. (See the following "Behaviors with Bailey" for the lowdown on this trick.)

Intrigued by my suggestion, I was asked to show the Farrelly Brothers what I had in mind ASAP. (Needing to get things done "yesterday" is the status quo in Hollywood, so I was prepared for the request.) I was thinking of a Border Terrier named Slammer, who was owned by another studio trainer. The look was right, the breed was perfect, and Slammer already had some necessary behaviors on her. She met the brothers and wowed them with her talent, and only two days passed before I received word that she was hired. At the same time, the brothers also instructed me to get a male Border Terrier to serve as back-up dog. Puffy was a boy, after all.

While I thought I was clever to come up with a Border Terrier in the first place, finding a second, identical dog posed a new, unexpected challenge. Border Terriers were not a particularly common breed at the time, so I was sweating, to say the least. Nevertheless, with some good connections and a little bit of luck, I quickly located a reputable Border Terrier breeder nearby. At the facility I met a litter of three, including a four-month-old dog I felt was a match. With only two months to prepare for the upcoming shoot in Miami, FL, we were cutting it close with a puppy, but I knew I could make it work.

Again, I not only found a home (mine) for our new back-up dog, Mouse, I immediately found homes for his brothers, too. I'm not kidding – finding homes for animals seems to be my special talent. In this case, one of the producers, Charlie Wessler, saw my adorable puppy and decided to buy his brother, whom he named Gort. Then a friend of mine bought the other brother. Hey breeders, here's my phone number... *Kathryn's Dog-Matching Service*... I only charge 10%!

Because the production crew had much preparation work to do in Florida before we arrived, Charlie asked me if I could keep Gort in Los Angeles and then bring him with me when I flew out with Mouse. I was concerned about watching both dogs, but my good friend Connie Light said she would take Gort instead. Connie, an animal expert, reasoned that if Gort stuck around with her, both he and Mouse would be house-trained by the time they got to Florida. What a score for Charlie, who was thrilled with the idea (who wouldn't be?). Connie came over frequently, so Gort and Mouse could play and learn together. They really enjoyed each other's company while mastering basic puppy obedience and potty training.

"Puffy" and "Magda"

Mouse's studio training also went very well. I worked with him on behaviors for about three hours throughout each day in random locations (to expose him to distractions), and he had everything down by the time we needed him to. That left only one final task before our trip to Florida: getting pictures and measurements taken at the special effects department. From that information, the special effects guys would make life-like stuffed dog that would be employed as stand-ins during lighting adjustments and in scenes where live dogs couldn't possibly be used. They also had to make the full-body cast Puffy wore in the movie after "Ted" inadvertently flings "Puffy" (the stuffed dog) out the window.

While at the special effects department, I had the pleasure of meeting Lin Shaye, the actress who played Puffy's sun-shriveled "mom" Magda. Just as the dogs were there getting measured for a body cast, the special effects team was taking Lin's measurements for a booby cast. Seriously! If you remember the movie, Matt Dillon's character, the bumbling private investigator, Healy, looks into what he thinks is gorgeous Mary's apartment through his binoculars. Instead of seeing Mary, however, he finds himself looking at Magda's "raisins!" Well, those "raisins" were unique to the character Magda. They were definitely not Lin's...

The scene brought the house down in every theater, but I'm sure most people didn't think about how the producers made it happen. Lin doesn't really look like a crazy, old, sunburned lady. In fact, she's beautiful. Her character in *There's Something About Mary* is an example of how special effects, along with the right script, actors, and crew, can truly pull off any illusion. In real life, Lin is an animal lover, proud mother, and stunning woman. It was so nice to meet her before we started working together as it gave me confidence to know the dogs would be performing with someone who truly cares for them.

The day Mouse and I travelled to Miami came and went uneventfully. On the plane Mouse sat quietly in his carrier, enjoying the flight. He acted as if flying were something he did every day. Of course, upon our arrival, the first order of business was a potty break (for both Mouse and me) before we were whisked away to the hotel in Coral Gables.

"Puffy" and Ben Stiller

At the hotel we were taken to a suite with a kitchen and balcony, and Mouse and I immediately began plotting to extend our stay. The room was so welcoming, and we knew that for the three months we were going to be there, it would feel just like home (but with room service - yum).

Connie soon flew in, and Charlie and Gort were happily reunited. After assisting me on the set for awhile, Connie returned to Los Angeles to help me handle my local clients while I was on location.

One dog who didn't need a hotel was the Great Dane I had also cast for the film. His role was to be the best friend of a snake, and I needed to find him in Miami (Great Danes don't quite make the cut to sit under the seat in front of me on the plane). I put the word out to trainers in Florida while I was still in Hollywood, asking to see their available dogs. They all knew the dog had to play nice with a snake, but every company except for one left that up to my imagination. One company actually sent a video of their dog with a snake, and of course, they got the job by a landslide.

Jules Sylvester's giant python

Our Great Dane now needed his best friend so we flew in the number one reptile wrangler in the world, Jules Sylvester, with his 20-foot-long python. Jules' experience comes from his childhood in the East African bush, where he was exposed to all things wild. By the age of 16, he was handling poisonous snakes at the Nairobi National Museum in Kenya and working on the TV series *Born Free*, which was filmed on his father's farm. It didn't take long for Jules to get the Hollywood bug, and he has since become one of the most sought after reptile wranglers, on and off camera. Needless to say, when I need a reptile on a show, I call Jules!

More so than any other film, while shooting *There's Something About Mary* I can remember many times when I needed to put my hand over my mouth so I wouldn't laugh-out-loud while shooting (so taboo). Everyone on the set was a dog lover, and Ben Stiller's performance with the dogs was definitely a highlight. He interacted with them so comically, yet so gently (if you can imagine him "gently" trying to shake a "vicious" dog off his leg). Cameron Diaz, Lee Evans, Jeffrey Tambor, and Matt Dillon all enjoyed the dogs, and Matt's nephew spent countless hours entertaining them (and himself). The best thing about the whole experience, however, is that between the battle scene with "Ted" and the French kissing scene with "Magda" (which almost beat out human kissing scenes at the MTV awards that year), Slammer and Mouse are two dogs who will never be forgotten.

I was out for a walk a few years ago, when I passed a woman walking a Border Terrier. I asked her about him, and she said she was visiting her mom, who owned the dog. She was surprised that I knew the breed, and when I told her about Mouse, she burst into laughter. It turns out that her mother chose a Border Terrier because of Puffy, or shall I say, because of Slammer and Mouse.

I'm glad the movie didn't cause Border Terrier-mania the way some movies do for other breeds. It always ends up that dogs of whatever the breed-of-the-day is get dumped at shelters when owners realize caring for them is actually work. The reason it didn't happen in this case is because Border Terriers are significantly more expensive than most other breeds, due to their scarcity. Still, I'm happy the girl's mom got a Border Terrier. Mouse was such a smart, trusting dog - I loved him, and I'm sure that woman's Border Terrier brought much joy to her life, too.

Mouse and Gort

Behaviors with Bailey – "Get It"

How great was the scene in *There's Something About Mary*, where Puffy drags Ted across the room by his pant leg? Want your dog to be able to drag your unwanted friend across the room? (I'm joking – only use this trick on people you like, it's not for violence.) Before I tell you how, please pay attention: this behavior should not be taught to small dogs (less than 15 lbs.) as it could injure them. Additionally, you should be sure to protect the leg or ankle you are going to teach your dog to go after in order to avoid injuries to the human "victim." This can be done with a neoprene under layer (like a brace), sports padding, or just some thick pants underneath the exposed pant leg.

Goal: To teach your dog to appear to be dragging a person across the room.

Number of Assistants: At least one.

Lesson:

- Start off using yourself as bait to maintain control of your dog.

- Put one of your dog's favorite toys under your pant leg so it is just visible.

- Shake your foot and say, "Get it."

- Praise your dog when they get the idea to shake up the toy within your pant leg. (The treat here will be letting your dog have the toy.)

Intermediate Challenge:

- Try the "get it" command again, but this time with the toy hidden all the way inside your pant leg.

Experts Only:

- Again, ask your dog to "get it," but this time with no toy up your pant leg. Have him "pull" you across the floor.

Tips:

- This behavior is easiest with dogs that are very toy-driven.

- The "get it" command can be dangerous if not taught properly. It is important your dog also understands the "leave it" command and lets go immediately when asked to.

Rhett in a European Esprit Ad

Obviously the dog world is full of strong bonds between humans and animals, but what about the bonds between humans with common dog interests? For me, many great friendships have been established as a result of my participation in dog shows, dog training, and other dog-related events. This is one of the things that make my job so fulfilling.

One such friendship was formed through a dog obedience club in the 1980's (I know, I'm dating myself). That's where I met Stephanie and Jim Gibbons, wonderful folks who bred the most beautiful Golden Retrievers on the West Coast. I was "Aunt Kathryn" to their amazing dogs, Rhett and Paddington, who were everyone's favorite Goldens. Photographers requested these top K9 models by name because they were not only stunning, they were also impeccably trained. Rhett and Paddington frequently appeared onscreen with big-name stars, like Tony Curtis (in a movie where they played search-and-rescue dogs) and Michael J. Fox (in a Japanese commercial). They were a dream to work with, although one shoot we did together almost turned into a nightmare.

Ironically, the job that almost killed me was a *Rescue 911* reenactment of a drowning boy who was saved by the family dog (a Golden Retriever). This shoot was on location at the Colorado River in Barstow, California, where the event actually occurred. The temperatures of the air and water couldn't have contrasted more - it was over 105 degree on land, but the water felt like it was freezing.

During the first day of shooting, we learned about the event first-hand from the family the story was about. They said their son, even after being told multiple times not to, was playing too close to the edge of the deck. As you have already guessed, he fell into the river, and their dog went in to rescue him. The boy had three child actors repeating his mistake for the cameras, and Rhett and Paddington were cast as the heroic family dog. That day the "boy" and his "dog" were filmed only on the deck – nobody actually went into the water (although there were several lifeguards supervising in case anyone fell in the river unexpectedly *again*).

The second day was the river shoot, and like the rough, roaring water, things got wild. Shooting the scene was especially challenging because of the fast current and burning sun, both of which made our work exhausting and precarious. The sequence of events was supposed to proceed as follows: boy falls in river; dog jump in after him; dog returns to me on land when I call him. That is, until the director called me over and said, "I really like how Rhett is jumping in, but he is looking in the wrong direction when he returns to you. Could you swim over to that boat and call him from there?"

I followed the director's gaze to an empty boat anchored across the river, and against my better judgment, I nodded. He then added the kicker, "By the way, we are out of lifejackets. You'll be able to hang onto the boat, though."

What? Who am I, Michael Phelps? My answer, of course, was, "Great!"

Swimming out to the boat was harder than I thought it would be, but I made it. I'm not kidding when I say the water was rough – hanging onto the side of the boat made me feel like driftwood whacking against a rock. While I floated, Stephanie placed Rhett and Paddington on a dock where the dogs would have a chance to rest between takes. I then called whichever dog whose turn it was, and it worked out exactly the way the director wanted it to.

Rhett and Paddington

By the time I heard, "LUNCH!" I had been in the water for more than 45 minutes, and hypothermia was setting in. Everyone bee-lined off the dock and headed for shore, grumbling stomachs causing them to forget I was out there. My legs were feeling numb, and I had to get out of the water, but pulling myself into the boat wasn't an option. I tried to swim for it, but as soon as I let go of the boat, I regretted my decision. The current seemed stronger than before, and since I was already exhausted, it easily dragged my helpless body downriver.

Stephanie saw what was happening and started screaming, "Someone, please, help Kathryn! She's going to drown!"

No one heard her, and for a second, I was a goner. Then, suddenly, Rhett and Paddington jumped in and swam towards me – it must have been déjà vu for the rescued boy's family. Each dog got under an arm and battled the current to swim me to shore. I couldn't believe it – Rhett and Paddington had just given a new meaning to the term "hero dog."

By the time we emerged from the water, the lifeguard was there waiting (sorry, bud, you missed your chance for heroics - I'm going home with the dogs). My legs were jelly and I couldn't stand, but other than that, I was fine. I probably wouldn't have been able to tell you about it now, had it not been for two wonderful Golden Retrievers.

Luckily the rest of the shoot was uneventful. Rhett and Paddington's bravery during my near-death experience most certainly had a lasting effect, though. The three of us had a bond before they saved my life, but afterward we were like glue. As for Stephanie and I, we were both so happy to have each other on that shoot, and our friendship will last a lifetime.

Behaviors with Bailey – "Head Down"

One thing the camera loves is facial expressions. Sometimes they are just there, but other times you have to make it happen. This is when having a "head down" behavior on your dog becomes very useful (*and it's oh so cute!*).

Goal: To teach your dog to look adorable – on command.

Lesson:

- 🐾 Put your dog in a down-stay.

- 🐾 With a treat in front of his nose, say, "Head down." Then have your dog follow your hand down to the ground.

- 🐾 When his head is down, pay him with the treat and lots of praise.

Intermediate Challenge:

- 🐾 Once your dog has mastered "head down" with a treat in front of his face, try teaching him to do it by just pointing down.

Experts Only:

- 🐾 Now that he is following your finger to the ground, see if you can teach your dog to turn his head towards his right or left leg by pointing towards either paw.

Tips:

- 🐾 If your dog is struggling to understand this behavior, put the hand that is not holding the treat gently on his head to guide it down (never push!).

Greg Louganis' beautiful Great Dane, Brutus – just before Greg and I made him black...

Being responsible for animals on a film set is a lot of fun, but it's also work. Like those who look after child actors, I must be focused on my charges and their specific needs first and foremost. To ensure their comfort, I always arrive earlier than my call time (that's the "biz" term for the time work begins) to find a comfortable area for my K9 actors to relax and rest. Sometimes I'll get a dressing room, but often I just need to stake a claim in a quiet hallway. If necessary, our home base can be my car (which is usually the case when we're on location).

K9 actors require an exercise pen when possible and a large crate or bed, where they can feel secure. Water and chew toys are essential, too. Before shooting, I only let the people who will actually be working with the dogs get to know them. I do this to minimize distractions and to help the dogs develop a relationship with their co-stars. After the shoot, it's party time, and everyone can say hello.

Chloe', relaxing while awaiting her call

Arriving on the set early enough for the dogs to acclimate, but not so early that boredom sets in, is a delicate balance I must maintain. Unless the role requires the dog to sleep, the most productive dogs are fresh and happy. Some roles, like the one Chloe' played in *Indecent Proposal*, call for both sleeping and waking scenes. Adrian, the director, was very understanding and always made sure we shot action scenes first. By the time it was late afternoon, and Chloe' had to play a sleeping dog under a kitchen table, she lay under the table and stopped acting – she was honestly fast asleep. As Woody and Demi recited their lines, Chloe' counted sheep (or

Picture This...

I'm on set with a Rottweiler who is about to greet Roseanne Barr with a terrifying set of teeth. She's playing a real estate agent showing a home, and my sweet, gentle Rottie is appearing as the neighbor's vicious dog.

The cameras roll, Roseanne walks past the house, and out pops a terrifying, barking, growling Rottweiler, exactly as expected. However, I don't think anyone let Roseanne in on the plan - I think I actually saw her heart stop for a second!

Remember when I said I like to introduce my dogs to the cast they'll be directly working with? For some reason the producers of this film thought it better not to. From now on I'm following my gut to save everyone wasted time and embarrassment. After a formal introduction to the very scary looking, but extremely nice Rottweiler, the scene was wrapped in a few takes and Roseanne was spared a second heart attack.

cats?)...and *snored!* As we held back our laughter, I gave Chloe' a light caress to curb her "enthusiam," and the two human actors carried on. Crisis averted, Chloe' was so pooped that, even when Adrian said, "Cut," she remained on her mark under the table.

In addition to having a calm space to retreat to, working with friends always puts me at ease. One of my favorite people to work with is Olympic diver, Greg Louganis. No, I don't have a hidden talent for diving. Greg's actually the one with the secret gift for showing Great Danes and training other dogs for agility. We met on the dog show circuit, where I couldn't but help notice how well-behaved his dogs were. When I got a call for a commercial that required one very large dog and one very small one, Greg's Great Dane Brutus was the first to come to mind (along with my Papillion, Checkers). The request was for white dogs, and since Checkers was white with red spots, and Brutus was a Harlequin (white with black spots), I knew they'd be the perfect fit. The producers agreed and we got the job.

The day of the shoot I met Greg and his dog at the studio. As always, I made sure to arrive early and set up a calm, happy environment for the dogs. Things always take a bit longer with Greg; everyone recognizes him and wants to meet him. I know to plan for it, though, and while he's chatting I check out our surroundings. When I looked around this particular set, I immediately discovered a BIG problem. The set was pure white...and so were the dogs! The camera wasn't even going to see them.

Once the commotion died down, Greg and I went out to get the dogs, and I alerted him of the issue. Sure enough, when we put the dogs in a sit-stay on the set, the director looked through the camera and saw *nothing*, except for some floating eyeballs and a few red and black spots. Surprised, the director asked me what to do, and within an hour I had his solution.

 Times like this are when I thank my lucky stars I learned Hollywood make-up in my early years. To this day I still always keep my make-up case with me. In Hollywood, you just never know when it might come in handy. So in the space of an hour, Greg and I ran the dogs back out to the van, gave them a complete makeover with black and brown pancake make-up, and had them back on the set, ready to shoot. Covering Brutus' face, chest, and front legs (the parts the camera would see) was an epic task. Checkers had much less surface area, but with longer hair, it was still quite the chore.

The tricks of the trade paid off this time, and the director commended us for our ingenuity. The shoot proceeded without further trouble, although make-up got all over the place. Greg, the dogs, and I were covered, and were all in need of a good scrubbing. I could go home and take my time washing up, but Greg had a Hollywood function to attend a few hours later. Our earlier "speed primping" caper did much to prepare Greg for this exact challenge, though. He rushed home, showered, and got to his event with minutes to spare. Such is "a day in life," in Hollywood.

Shoots, like the one Greg and I did together, reaffirm the importance of the quiet space I always set up for the dogs. After all the crazy scrambling on the set that day, I was happier than ever that the dirty dogs and I had a place to retreat to. When animals are involved, there is always some degree of uncertainty. By having their crates, water, food, and toys on hand, I can ensure the dogs are happy and ready to fetch whatever kind of curveball Hollywood throws our way.

Behaviors with Bailey – "On Your Feet"

Ever want to teach your dog to dance? Here's a good place to begin. Most studio trainers refer to "on your feet" as a dog standing on all fours, but obedience trainers call that a "stand." Because I have a background in obedience, I prefer to use "on your feet" when asking my dogs to stand on their *hind legs*. Honestly, it doesn't really matter. You can say "pickle" for all your dog cares – the important thing is that you remain consistent with whatever word or phrase you use.

Goal: To teach your dog to stand on his back legs.

Lesson:

- 🐾 Have your dog sit in front of you and hold some bait in front of his nose.

- 🐾 Move your hand up in front of him while saying, "On your feet."

- 🐾 Once on his hind legs, praise your dog and pay him.

    Intermediate Challenge:

- 🐾 Once your dog knows "on your feet" like the back of his paw, try moving your hand in a circle as you raise it while saying, "Dance." Did he twirl around in a circle?

Tips:

- 🐾 It tends to be easier to teach Toy and small breed dogs this trick because standing on their back legs is not particularly difficult for them.

- 🐾 Always consider your dog's size and weight for behaviors like "on your feet." If your dog is overweight or very large, this behavior may be unsafe for him.

- 🐾 If your dog is very toy-motivated, you may be able to teach this behavior using a toy instead of treats or food.

- 🐾 Do not teach this behavior to your dog if he has any medical problems that cause him leg or back pain.

Buster: "I'm not scruffy, am I?"

Dog Magnet

While on a shoot in downtown Los Angeles, I took my K9 actor out for a walk. We hadn't gone far when a filthy, starving, four-month-old puppy ran up to us and followed us back to the set. The crew knew the dog; he'd come to "base camp" every day for a week, scavenging for food and water. They had gone around the neighborhood trying to find his home, and after meeting him, I stepped into the detective role. I was equally unsuccessful, and it quickly became apparent that this puppy had been dumped.

With no other choice, I took the dog home, named him Buster, and gave him a bath. I had no idea what color he was until all the dirt ran down the drain (turned out he wasn't brown). He lived with me as a foster until a group that trains dogs for the hearing impaired contacted me. They evaluated Buster for their program, checking out his intelligence and hearing, and he passed with flying colors. Six months into his training they called me with an update – the scruffy dog, who found me on the streets, had graduated first in his class! He was placed with a family in which the mother and father were hearing impaired and needed Buster's help. His job was to know the difference between telephone, doorbell, and tea kettle sounds (among others), and then lead his owners to the right thing. Buster had found the best of both worlds (work and play) because he had a job to do, and his family had a son for him to play with when he wasn't working. It was truly a "happily ever after" ending for a life that was almost consumed by the lonely Los Angeles streets.

I seem to be a magnet for dogs in need. I don't know if it's the treats I carry or just the vibe I give off, but it's fine with me. Finding the right home for a wayward pup is one of the most rewarding things I can do. While working on *Indecent Proposal*, not only did I find homes for Chloe' and several other dogs at the Burbank Shelter, I also rescued a litter of puppies from the L.A. Shelter. They were so cute that one wasn't enough for Demi Moore, she couldn't resist taking two.

Invariably, when I'm on the set working as a studio animal trainer, someone comes to me with a litter of puppies or a dog that needs a home. And somehow we always find good homes, be it with stars, crew, or friends. On the flipside, I never worry that the dogs won't be loving enough towards their new owners; every rescue dog I've known has been big on gratitude.

Sometimes the line between my "official" job and rescue work is blurred, as was the case the summer I spent at Woods Humane Society in San Luis Obispo. Woods hosts a day camp where kids and homeless dogs are paired up to learn from each other. I found out about it because my step-brother, Paige, and his wife, Karen, sent their sons, Matt and Andy.

The program teaches children the proper care and handling of dogs, and dogs learn obedience and companionship. I led the basic obedience classes with the help of my Papillion, Scarlett. And on the last day of camp, my reward was to watch the kids show off their newfound skills for the parents. The result of this "show" was that many families adopted the dogs their children were working with, which is exactly what Paige's family did. It's a brilliant program and everybody goes home happy. Even the dogs who are not immediately adopted tend to find families quickly because they have already been loved and trained.

While I was teaching at Woods, Scarlett hit it off with a camp counselor's Dachshund. The following year a charity event was planned, where Scarlett and the Dachshund were to be "married." What a hoot! Out of all of the crazy animal-related requests I've received in my life, getting a wedding gown for Scarlett and a tux for the Dachshund still takes the cake to this day.

After the "wedding," the charity event wound down, and I began loading up my car. Just as I was ready to leave, a car pulled up next to me, and out popped a woman with a litter of puppies. She told me that she had found them hiking and had first brought them to her local shelter. Upon learning that the dogs would be euthanized because they were too young to care for or adopt out, she decided to try Woods. However, when she arrived at Woods' shelter, she found a sign directing her to the doggie park (which brought her to me). This kind-hearted woman couldn't seem to get a break that day!

As the woman shared her story, bystanders began to take an interest in the seven puppies. Six were black and one was a wheaten color – so cute, and apparently healthy, too. *Hey, how did the wheaten one suddenly end up in my arms?* Three people each took a puppy, which left four still needing homes (including the wheaten). The Woods office was closed for the night so the puppies were out of luck, and I'm still not sure how it happened, but suddenly everyone was gone, and there I stood with four puppies.

I was able to track down someone on the Woods' staff, who said I should bring the pups by the next morning. They would call their foster families and arrange for appropriate care, but that still left the dogs homeless for the night. During that week, I was staying with my father, a real lover of all things furry, so of course, the dogs went home that night with me.

When my father and I arrived at Woods the following day, we were greeted by good news and bad news, or so it seemed at the time. The good news was that fosters were found for three puppies. The bad news was that still left an odd dog out.

Bailey

Noooo.... I didn't need another dog. I had Scarlett, who was six at the time, and I still wasn't over the loss of Chloe'. The people at Woods knew, and I knew, that if the wheaten-colored puppy got in my car to come home and be "fostered" that day, she would stay there forever. And so, the bad news turned into the best news for that pup. For nine years now, her name has been Bailey. She grew into a 60+ lb. Lab mix who thinks she is a Toy Breed, and she has done some print and commercial work. She's got that lovable family dog look, which comes as no surprise. She's a lovable family dog!

Having been owned by several talented, mixed-breed dogs, I'm very excited about an American Kennel Club (AKC) rule that has recently been revised. For years, all breeds (pure and mixed) have been allowed to test for the AKC's Canine Good Citizen (CGC) Award, which is one platform for becoming a Therapy Dog. However, now mixed-breed dogs can also compete in AKC obedience, agility, and rally events. Bailey and her buddies say, "Woof, woof, bark!"(Thanks, AKC!).

Competing in AKC events is only one way to have fun with a rescued dog. Obviously many well-trained, mixed-breed rescues have found themselves on TV, in print, and on stage. Photographers, directors, and casting agents are always looking for dogs all over the country. With patience and persistence, your dog could become famous, too! If you wanted to pursue that route, you could call local photographers, theater companies, and schools, to see if they need a dog for anything. Another option is to start a party business. People might hire you and your dog to perform at birthday parties, town fairs, and other events.

Making your dog famous is not really what's important though, is it? Does your dog make you smile? Has he or she helped you, or others, through tough times, just by being there? These dogs, the ones that bring so much joy to our lives, are already K9 stars!

The "nudge" is a fun behavior because it makes your dog use his brain.

Goal: To teach your dog to nudge an object.

Lesson:

- 🐾 Put a lightweight cup upside-down on the floor with a treat underneath it (don't let your dog see you set it up).

- 🐾 As soon as you dog figures out the reward is under the cup, he'll start pushing it to get the treat. When he does, say, "Nudge it."

- 🐾 Once the treat is retrieved, praise him!

Intermediate Challenge:

- 🐾 Once your dog has the idea, ask him to nudge other things, like people and stuffed animals.

Scout, aka "Air Bud," from the movie "Air Buddies"

A Pup Takes Flight

One day, a beautiful Golden Retriever puppy walked into my studio training class. His human parents, Khaki and Scott McKee, had just moved to Southern California from back East and wanted to train their dog, Scout. He was about a one-and-a-half years old, and like most Goldens, a real lover and a smarty-pants.

Four or five weeks into class, I received a call from another studio trainer, who would be working on the next *Air Bud* film for Disney. She asked me if I knew of any well-trained, male Goldens, and the first dog I thought of was Scout. He was young, but then again, so was Chloe' when she did *Indecent Proposal*, and her youth wasn't an issue at all. Even though he'd only completed the first part of the three-part training program, I was convinced that with some preparation, Scout was up to the task.

I discussed the opportunity with Khaki and Scott, and we all decided it was worth a try. We sent my trainer friend a photo of Scout and were shocked to receive word that they hired him, simply based on his photo and description. (Being cast without even an audition is something that very rarely happens.) Scout was to be the hero dog, "Air Bud," in the film *Air Buddies*. It's not just human unknowns who get their big break in Hollywood – dogs, cats, snakes, giraffes, you name it – they can get their big break, too!

I was unable to go to Canada for the filming, which was unfortunate, because the production company had rented a beautiful house on a river for the dogs and trainers. It was perfect for water-loving Golden Retrievers (which were in *abundance* on the set). Khaki and Scott did get to go, and they reported back that they were happy Scout had been through some agility training with me. In one of the scenes he had to run through a tunnel, and he got it in one or two takes.

Since the movie, Scout has continued his acting career with print and commercial work. Sears Optical liked him so much that they used him for one entire TV and print campaign. As usual, Scout performed his role with the greatest of ease – he shot the print shoot one day and the commercial shoot the next. Some dogs would be beat after two long days of work, but not Scout. He's always ready for more.

Scout kayaking with mom and dad

Scout's a happy, attentive, loving dog because he lives with an equally happy, attentive, loving family. Khaki and Scott were never in the "biz" but have enjoyed watching their fur-kid thrive. They make sure he doesn't work too much, and spend plenty of time playing with him in the California surf. They also guide him to use his star power to raise awareness and funding for Golden Retriever rescues. Unlike some humans, Scout's stardom hasn't gone to his head – he's always happy to lend a helping paw to his brothers and sisters in need.

Did You Know?

Golden Retrievers and Labrador Retrievers are the two breeds most frequently requested for commercial shoots.

Scout in a Sears Optical ad

Behaviors with Bailey – "Go With"

"Go with" is a good behavior to have on your dog, whether or not he does studio work. It comes in handy anywhere your dog may need to go somewhere with another person, like the veterinary office or grooming salon.

Goal: To teach your dog to walk away with another person, upon your command, without looking back at you.

Required Number of Assistants: One

Lesson:

- Give your helper some bait, and tell her that you are going to walk your dog over to her, hand her the leash, and then she should walk away with your dog.

- Start at the opposite side of the room, and walk your dog on-leash to your helper.

- Hand your helper the leash, and as she walks away with your dog, say, "Go with."

- Keep practicing until your dog will walk with the other person without looking back at you.

Intermediate Challenge:

- Have your dog practice with many different helpers so your dog understands to obey your command, regardless of who he is walking with.

Experts Only:

- Can your dog "go with" off leash? Without the leash but in a safe environment, have your helper hold a treat where you dog can see it, lead your dog up to your helper, and then say, "Go with," as they walk away together. Did it work? If not, try alternating between on-leash and off-leash attempts.

Tips:

- Have your helper show your dog the treat in her hand.

- Let your helper know to pay your dog once he is walking comfortably with her.

- Give your dog lots of praise once he returns to you.

Checkers playing with a piglet

Things just fell into place with Scout, but finding the right dog for a part isn't always easy. The task becomes especially cumbersome when the humans involved forget that dogs are not battery-operated. One time the producers of a sitcom invited me to audition a small dog for a role requiring a few basic behaviors, including playing dead. I told them my Papillion, Checkers, had the right look and all of the behaviors except the dead dog, which I could teach him in a few days. They said to bring him in anyway, with or without the dead dog behavior.

I took Checkers to meet the production team, and he impressed them with his skills - minus the dead dog. They loved him, and then asked, "So, does he do a dead dog?"

Had I been talking to myself earlier that day? I answered, "As I mentioned, he doesn't have a dead dog on him just yet. I can teach it to him in a few days."

I kid you not, their next comment was, "Are you sure?" I'm sure – my dog does not have a reprogrammable circuit board, and I can't change his batteries - but it wouldn't have helped to say that. Sometimes you have to just show people, so I pulled a stuffed dog out of my bag, tossed it across the room, and yelled, "Play dead!" When it landed, it gave the producers the brilliant performance my dog was not able to give at the time. It got a good laugh, and a, "We'll call you." We didn't get the job, but our audition reminded them that, if they want a dog to play dead who hasn't been trained on the behavior, they might as well get a stuffed one. I'm known to be an experienced trainer, but nobody is that good.

JJ, the One Take Wonder

On any shoot, my dogs and I need to be flexible and ready for anything. Sometimes the directors stick to the script, but occasionally they look to us to improvise. A few of years ago I helped my colleague Candy's Jack Russell Terrier, JJ, land a part on the soap opera *General Hospital*. He played a dog that was lost and running all over town. JJ's performance blew everyone's minds and earned him the nickname "One Take Wonder." (As I mentioned earlier, each time a scene is shot it's called a "take." Obviously, being able to do it in one take is very good!)

The director had so much faith in JJ that he added a scene where JJ had to run through a maze. Candy and I patterned him, or walked him through it, twice – that's all it took with JJ. When the director said "Action," I released JJ and Candy called him. The scene was a wrap. JJ received a standing ovation and we got a pat on the back. We had definitely nailed that one in terms of finding the right dog for the right part. No reprogramming necessary.

"Cover" is a behavior that is used to show a dog's embarrassment, not that your dog would ever actually do this on his own! However, it is endearing for humans and always gets a laugh on screen or at parties. This is a behavior you can really have a lot of fun with.

Goal: To teach your dog to cover his eyes with his paw.

Lesson:

- This is going to sound crazy, but *lightly* place some removable tape on your dog's face.

- Stand back, and watch your dog try to remove the tape.

- As your dog is pawing his face, say, "Cover."

- After a while, your dog will get the idea and you will no longer need the tape.

- Don't forget to praise your dog!

Reviewing a call sheet – when on set it's important to know when and where to be, and where not to be!

Setiquette

Studio trainers spend the majority of their time striving to remain unnoticed. Even a *good* K9 performance is worthless if the viewer (whether it's a television audience, movie-goer, or magazine reader) can tell a trainer is present off-camera. The dogs must look as natural as the humans and not reveal that they are actually taking cues from someone (named Kathryn) in the darkness.

Becoming a good studio trainer takes a lot of thought, time, and preparation. I was lucky because my parents guided me and shared their TV and movie set experience with me, but not everyone has that luxury. People looking to break into the business need to understand that having well-trained dogs is only one part of the equation. Professionalism, and especially understanding the do's and don'ts of set etiquette, is what will get you a call back for a job.

As with anything, there is a right way and a wrong way of being on a set. It is easy to do things the wrong way, drawing the bad kind of attention to yourself. For example, a roped-off set is a "hot set." The right thing to do is to leave it undisturbed. The wrong thing to do is to go and eat the cookies that have been strategically placed on the table for the upcoming shoot. I can see you thinking, "That's easy, who's going to go and eat some random cookies left on a table?" Remember – as a studio trainer I have a dog (or dogs) with me, and for them, abandoned cookies are hard to resist. Being on a set with animals requires extra diligence. Above and beyond being aware of my own actions, I always need to be vigilant about the dogs.

For some people, being on a set, and learning all of the rules and norms, can be very awkward. Not for JJ's mom Candy – she is a born natural. The *General Hospital* shoot we did together, with JJ, was her first union job. She had done other shows and student films with her dogs, but with *General Hospital* she found herself having to learn a new set of rules and guidelines as required by the Union. You see, all of the major soap operas, and most

Picture This...

I'm in a van with another trainer, a dog, and five crates of homing pigeons, on my way to a commercial shoot. At the studio gate, the following conversation ensues:

Guard: Name and ID, please.
Me: Here you go.
Guard: Where are you going?
Me: Stage six, commercial shoot.
Guard: What will you be doing there? (Okay, I know he saw the birds and the dog.)
Me: We're the caterers.
Guard: Have a good day! (He opens the gate and lets us through.)

Don't get any ideas, my name was on the list. If it hadn't been we might still be at the gate discussing the day's lunch menu – pigeon stew (Ewww...)!

network television shows, for that matter, require everyone on a set to be part of a union. There are too many unions to list, but the one that governs animal wranglers is Local 399. To do the shoot, Candy had to become a union member, which meant finding a sponsor within the union and apprenticing for 30 days. This was no problem for Candy. I gladly sponsored her, and we had a great time working together.

When a trainer doesn't play by the rules or acts inappropriately, it gets around. The tabloids aren't the only place to find gossip; in Hollywood it spreads like wildfire. Candy once related a story to me about another trainer she worked with on a commercial shoot who spent the entire day yelling at her and JJ. The yelling didn't go over so well and resulted in poor JJ, the dog who would become known as the One Take Wonder, shutting down. This reflected poorly on JJ and Candy, but it was an especially black mark against the trumpeting trainer, and everyone surely heard about it. These lessons are important for me to hear, and I take them with me as a reminder of what to do, and what not to do, when on a set. (Although, it sounded to me like that particular trainer's problem went well beyond understanding appropriate setiquette. Maybe she needed some behavior classes for herself!)

Behaviors with Bailey – "Whistle Recall"

Teaching your dog "whistle recall" is very useful – especially if you ever go out to a field or dog park where he may get far enough away from you that he can't hear your voice. To teach this behavior, you'll need bait, a whistle, and a long, loose leash.

Goal: To teach your dog to return to you when you whistle.

Lesson:

- 🐾 Let your dog get as far away from you as your leash will allow him.

- 🐾 Blow your whistle and step back, gently tugging on the leash to give your dog the idea that he should come to you.

- 🐾 As soon as your dog gets to you, pay him with your bait and a lot of praise.

- 🐾 Repeat several times.

Intermediate Challenge:

- 🐾 Take your dog off leash in a safe environment, and continue practicing whistle recall with him.

Experts Only:

- 🐾 Get an assistant and an extra whistle, and go out to a large, safe field where your dog can run around.

- 🐾 Instruct your assistant to go to the far end of the field with a whistle, and blow it once she is there.

- 🐾 When she blows the whistle, release your dog. The idea is for your dog to run to your assistant.

- 🐾 Once he is with your assistant, call your dog back to you by blowing your whistle. Not only is this a fun activity for you and your dog, but it's a great way to give your dog exercise.

Dogs sell.

Dogs Sell

12

The next time you sit down to watch your favorite TV show, pay attention to the commercials. How many of them include a dog? I think the answer will surprise you. Whether the product or service is pet-related or not (like a home security company wanting to emphasize that their system keeps the *whole* family safe - including the dog), dogs *sell*. For this I am grateful - if I were a dog, commercials would be my bushes and trees. I've done so many that it's hard to keep them straight. A few, however, are memorable…

McDonald's requested wolves for a European commercial. They wanted ten, to be exact, sitting on a mountain, each a foot apart from one another, in the presence of a mountain man. Let me begin by saying that although I've got some pretty extensive resources, ten "trained" wolves are simply not something I come across every day. Additionally, what sort of "Hollywood" mountain man is going to perform "naturally" in the presence of ten wild animals? He's more likely to be peeing himself. Wolves are NOT dogs – while they can be trained, humans amidst a pack of "trained" wolves can still quickly turn into something that would be shown on Discovery instead of a McDonald's commercial, if you know what I mean.

I thought a safer, easier alternative would be to round up one wolf and nine Malamutes, and after making my case with the help of some convincing photographs, the producers agreed. I knew of a very well-trained wolf that would be perfect for the part. He was socialized with dogs and humans, so we hired him.

The Malamutes came from a different owner, who knew there would be a wolf on the set but apparently hadn't prepared himself psychologically. The day of the shoot started out fine - I gave a safety talk, informing cast and crew that they were not to go near the wolf, with or without a dog, unless I was supervising and it was part of the shoot. Next, I positioned all of the dogs, and once they were calm and knew their marks, I brought in the wolf.

Wolf used in the McDonald's commercial shoot

Everyone was doing great until the owner of the Malamutes became nervous. This is the worst thing any owner can do in a tense situation because the dogs pick up on it immediately. His anxiety quickly transferred to his dogs and lips started rising with canines showing. At that moment, our shoot could have wrapped with a scene from *When Animals Attack*, but I knew I had a choice: I could also pick up on the owner's anxiety and start panicking, or I could remain calm and give a little pep-talk to the humans and canines. Of course, it wasn't really a decision. Experience led me to choose the latter, so I reminded everyone how their *calm* feelings would reassure the dogs and spent a few minutes petting the animals. In no time at all, we were back in action.

The shoot went well from there, but the irony is that the big, bad wolf was really not an issue, and had the dogs been left in a room with him alone, there probably would have been no tension at all. As humans, we really need to be aware of our feelings around animals – our animals are often a reflection of ourselves!

Talk about bizarre, I once received a call from a producer I had worked with numerous times before, apologizing that she hadn't hired me first for her current shoot and asking me if I would consider stepping in. As the story goes, the client insisted on using a trainer that was a friend of his, but she had been difficult from the start. First, the trainer requested a week of prep time, which is the time it takes to train a dog for the necessary behaviors (during which, I might add, the trainer gets paid full day rate and the dog gets paid half rate). For complicated behaviors this is understandable, but when I asked what she was training her dog to do I couldn't believe my ears. *She was training the dog to wag his tail!*

The story doesn't end there. When the trainer in question arrived on the set with her dog, she looked around, stopped dead in her tracks, and said, "I'm sorry, but the vibe is all wrong here. My dog won't work under these conditions." With that she walked off the stage and out the door - never to be seen again. The poor cast and crew were abruptly left without their star, but I knew I could help. I asked the producer, "When do you need me?"

She said, "Now, with a dog that wags his or her tail." This wasn't a tall order, so I immediately called a friend and we took four dogs down so they could pick the look they wanted. The director's eyes lit up when he saw the dogs because they were *already* wagging their tails – what a concept! He quickly made his choice, and then asked if the dog could mop the floor. *What?* Why didn't I think of that sooner? We should train all of the shelter dogs to mop floors and then they'll be adopted immediately! The man was obviously serious so I thought about it for a second and came up with a plan.

We put a large sponge on the floor and showed the dog it was his mark. Once he put his paws on the "mark," we asked him to hold it, and then gave him a "slow come" command. It worked, and actually made it appear as though he were cleaning the floor. Now we had something to show off, and it didn't take me a week of prep!

I opened the stage door to find the crew staring at me with fear in their eyes. What had this other woman done to them? I knew I had to put them at ease, and fast. But how? The answer was spontaneous. I said, "Oh, no, this isn't going to work. I was promised burning incense. I'm sorry, this is just wrong." The crew looked like they were either going to walk out of the room or throw up, so I quickly said, "Just kidding!" Everyone laughed and immediately knew we were on the level – my dog and I were there to get the job done, and we didn't have any goofy set requirements. The dog performed brilliantly, finishing his task in a minimal number of takes, and we got a bonus for saving the day and leaving the floor spotless!

One of the most beautiful settings for a commercial shoot has to be the Malibu, CA surf. Rhett, and another one of Stephanie's dogs, Missy, were to do a reenactment of a scene from the movie *From Here to Eternity* for a Swedish commercial. It called for the dogs to roll in the surf, which was especially challenging because the water was very rough. Regardless, Rhett loves water and went right in. My task was to put both dogs in a down-stay. Sitting there with the waves coming in and not breaking their positions, took a lot of love and trust, but Rhett and Missy did great! In fact, they pulled it off so well that the commercial gained fame on the international stage as one of the best commercials shot that year.

As an aside, shortly after the Swedish commercial job, Rhett and Missy had a litter. It's not just human stars that have kids that get into showbiz. Rhett and Missy's pup, Lucky, took over many jobs for his aging "father" once he was full grown. He even got to do a print ad with Rod Stewart! Lucky was just that – lucky – but he was also very talented and he went on to have a great career.

Rhett's "son" Lucky in an ad with Rod Stewart

Behaviors with Bailey – "Give Paw"

Everybody loves a dog that can give a high-five, which is a popular behavior to teach. Here's how you can teach your dog to give a high-five, and then turn that high-five into a wave!

Goal: To teach your dog to give you his paw and also to wave.

Lesson:

- 🐾 Have your dog sit in front of you with a collar on (no chokers!).

- 🐾 Stand in front of him and put your hands close to his neck.

- 🐾 Put your right hand out towards your dog's right paw, and say, "Give paw," while at the same time gently pulling his collar to the left to tip him slightly off balance. (Don't pull hard, just pull enough to get your dog to pick up his right paw.)

- 🐾 Touch his paw and praise him, accompanied by a treat if necessary.

Intermediate Challenge:

- 🐾 Once your dog knows how to "give paw," try it with the opposite paw by saying, "Give foot," and repeating the steps on the opposite side.

Experts Only:

- 🐾 A more advanced version of asking for your dog's paw is to ask him to wave. Put your dog on a sit-stay, step back, and put your hand out as if to shake his paw.

- 🐾 As soon as the dog's paw comes up, say, "Wave."

- 🐾 Praise your dog and pay him. Dogs are very smart, and will quickly pick up on the difference between "paw" and "wave."

The current "Rusty," Natural Balance spokesdog and local hero

Everyone thinks of Hollywood as a place where there is a lot of "getting" going on. People get money, cars, fame, fortune – but what is not often seen is how much "giving" occurs as well. Just like any small town, Hollywood is a place where people look out for each other, care for each other, and help out however we can.

Terry Wainscott, the owner of Rusty's Discount Pets where I have been shopping for 22 years, is a perfect example of the heart of Hollywood. Terry always helps rescue organizations by hosting events and then donating proceeds. His Halloween fundraiser event gets better every year. Adults, kids, and their dogs come to the store dressed in Halloween costumes. I photograph them and a panel of judges votes for the winner. People love it! (We do something similar at Christmas, too.)

Last year we had an unusually cold winter, and mountains that don't often get snow were dumped on. Linda Blair, child star of *The Exorcist* and founder of the WorldHeart Foundation (a Pit Bull rescue), was snowed in and desperately needed blankets, towels, and beds for her foster dogs. Rusty's rallied to help both the WorldHeart Foundation and the South Los Angeles Shelter, ensuring a merry Christmas for dogs that may have otherwise died.

Terry loves supporting rescue and will continue to host philanthropic events. What goes around, comes around, and Terry has had his fair share of good fortune, as well. When one "Rusty" crosses the bridge, Terry gets another, and they are always wonderful dogs. The current "Rusty," is a beautiful, rough coat, sable and white Collie who I schooled on some studio behaviors. His beauty was not lost on the marketers at Dick Van Patten's Natural Balance, a natural dog food company that also has a soft spot for rescue, and the current Rusty is now one of the dogs featured in their ads.

Behaviors with Bailey – "Crate Training"

There is nothing more important than helping your dog feel at ease in a crate. Some people think crate training is cruel, but any behaviorist knows that dogs are den animals who appreciate a place where they can have some quite time and feel safe. At some point in your dog's life, he will surely find himself in a crate – whether it is at the vet, groomer, or when traveling in a car or airplane. By crate training your dog, you can ensure that these experiences are as comfortable as can be.

Goal: To teach your dog to see his crate as a safe, happy place.

Lesson:

- 🐾 Put your dog's crate in the room where you spend most of your time with a comfortable blanket inside it.

- 🐾 Make sure the door is open and can't close when your dog enters (block the door open if necessary - if the door hits him as he enters, he'll hate it right away).

- 🐾 Put some treats or your dog's food in the back of the crate, and encourage him to explore with the door open.

- 🐾 Praise him softly when he goes in.

- 🐾 When your dog feels comfortable enough you may close the door.

Tips:

- 🐾 Don't make a big deal out of the crate – your dog picks up on your emotions, so if you are nonchalant about it, he will be too.

- 🐾 Never leave you dog in a crate for longer than 3 hours at a time, unless it's over night.

Chloe', my sweet dreams dog

That's a Wrap

In closing, I'd like to say thanks to my sweet Chloe', who so deeply touched my life. This poem by my mother says it all:

Have you ever seen a large white misty cloud, soundlessly enter a room so hardly to be noticed? That was Chloe'.

Have you ever known the selfless and unconditional love of a dog who throws herself on her beloved friend to protect her from an earthquake? That was Chloe'.

Can you imagine this beautiful Labrador mix, so appreciative having been rescued from the pound, more than willing to listen and learn everything her new friend taught her, to become a movie dog within two weeks from pound to cameras? That was Chloe'.

Then maybe you can try to understand how she could suffer with a genetic disease and cancer without ever complaining. That was Chloe'.

Now you will believe that she knew when her young life was ending, as she arduously dragged all eighty-six pounds of herself into to the room where she chose to die, a room where she knew she would be surrounded by love from her two-legged and four-legged family members. That was Chloe'.

Don't be surprised then, when I tell you that she was so close to God, her best friend, her human "mother," placed holy water on her forehead while praying that the Lord would free her from her pain. Within minutes, her prayers were answered.

If ever there could be a canine saint in heaven... It would be Chloe'.

By Christie Rhodes

No humans were harmed in the writing of this book
(but we did kill one computer)

Photo Credits

Cover/Interior Title: Indecent Proposal, Chloe' and Woody/ Paramount Pictures

5: Phil Segura/Paramount Pictures

8: Lin Shaye & Mouse/Phil Segura

10: Lin Shaye/Stephanie Yantz, Instinct Magazine

12: Bailey, Holly & Kathryn Segura/Pam Marks, Paw Prince Studios

16: Commercial Shoot/ Kathryn Segura

18: Rin Tin Tin/Chappel Bros., Inc. Ken-L-Ration

20: Ace/Kathryn Segura

23: Ace/Phil Segura

28: Tasha/Phil Segura

30: Tasha/Kathryn Segura

31: Tasha/Kathryn Segura

34: Bailey/Kathryn Segura

36: USA WEEKEND/Kathryn Segura

38: Jon/Kathryn Segura

42: Bailey/Kathryn Segura

44: Indecent Proposal/Paramount Pictures

47: Chloe' at make-up table/Phil Segura

48: Woody & Chloe'/Paramount Pictures

52: Puffy& Cameron Diaz/Kathryn Segura

54: Puffy & Magda/ Phil Segura

55: Ben Stiller/Kathryn Segura

56: Jules Sylvester's giant python/Kathryn Segura

57: Mouse & Gort/Kathryn Segura

58: Mouse w/ shark/Phil Segura

60: Rhett Esprit Ad/Peggy Sirota

62: Rhett and Paddington/Kathryn Segura

64: Bailey and Holly/Kathryn Segura

66: Brutus/Kathryn Segura

67: Chloe'/Phil Segura

70: Mouse/ Kathryn Segura

72: Buster/Kathryn Segura

75: Bailey/Pam Marks, Paw Prince Studios

77: JJ/Candy Clemente

78: Scout/Khaki McKee

80: Scout, Khaki, and Scott McKee/Les Hardwick

82: Woody Harrleson and Chloe'/Paramount Pictures

84: Checkers/Kathryn Segura

86: JJ/Dana Maione

87: JJ/Candy Clemente

88: Kathryn Segura/Anne Oakner

92: Scout/Khaki McKee

94: Kathryn Segura

96: Kathryn Segura

98: Rod Stewart & Lucky/Kathryn Segura

100: Lucky/Kathryn Segura

102: Rusty/Terry Wainscott

104: Bailey and Holly/Kathryn Segura

106: Chloe'/Phil Segura

111: Kathryn Segura/Pam Marks, Paw Prince Studios

About Kathryn Segura

After a childhood full of dog shows and a stint in the high fashion make-up industry, Kathryn Segura found her niche in Hollywood as a studio wrangler/animal trainer. Through her company *PHD Animals*, she has helped cast and train every creature imaginable: from cats to dogs, horses to zebras, and even "lions, tigers, and bears" (Oh, my!). With a resume chock full of experience in print work, TV shows and series, commercials, and major motion pictures (such as the blockbuster hits discussed in this book, *Tin Cup*, and *The Addams Family*), Kathryn continues to be called upon to bring life and depth to "anything Hollywood." Recently, Kathryn has melded her passion for animals with her experience in fashion and make-up to create *Take 1 Products*, which makes specialized animal skin and fur care products.

Buy a "Lost Souls: Found!" Book and Support Your Favorite Breed Rescue

Schnauzer Chihuahua Golden Retriever PUG
DACHSHUND German Shepherd Collie Boxer
Labrador Retriever Husky Beagle ALL AMERICAN
Border Collie Pit Bull Terrier Shih Tzu Miniature Pinscher
Chow Chow Australian Shepherd Rottweiler Greyhound
Boston Terrier Jack Russell Poodle Cocker Spaniel
GREAT DANE Doberman Pinscher Yorkie SHEEPDOG
ST. BERNARD Pointer Blue Heeler

The Happy Tails Books™ "Lost Souls: Found!" series showcases the love and joy adopted dogs bring to their new homes. Organized by breed, the series was created to help support animal rescue efforts by educating readers about rescue, breed characteristics, and the proper care and training of dogs. Have you adopted a dog? Submit your own story or pick up a book about your favorite breed today!

Happy Tails Books™ donates a significant portion of proceeds back to the rescue groups who help gather stories for the books.

Happy Tails Books™

To submit a story or learn about other books Happy Tails Books™ publishes, please visit our website at http://happytailsbooks.com